WHAT ABOUT THE CHURCH?

Is it still relevant? Necessary? Or for ancient times?

BY SUHAINA BENILIA - SOPHIA

PUBLIC TRANSFORMATION
THE NETHERLANDS

WHAT ABOUT THE CHURCH?
by Suhaina Benilia-Sophia

Published by
PUBLIC TRANSFORMATION,
Moerkapelle, The Netherlands

ISBN: 9789083083360
NUR: 707

Public Transformation – For Books with Impact!

I dedicate this book to my God and Creator, the One who inspired me to write this book.

To my husband, Swendly, thank you for being who you are: loving, consistent, and supportive.

To my mother, Zulaica, your hard work and love have brought me this far.

To my publisher, Stefan, thank you for the help, guidance, and making this a reality.

Table of Contents

Foreword

It was probably in 2012 that I met Suhaina in church, where my wife and I were actively involved. At that time, I remember her being very kind, attentive, and a little introverted or even shy. She was attending the Alpha course and was involved in the youth ministry. We didn't connect until 2016, when my wife and I were asked to lead the church she was part of. After a few rocky months where, unfortunately, many congregants and leaders left, we launched a new church in October 2016 and started our journey together.

As her pastor, my wife and I were quick to notice her passion for the Word of God and her willingness to be taught. We started building relationship and not long after, she was appointed a deacon in the church. Her serving heart and hunger for the Word of God increased in the years after, and we prayerfully appointed her as an elder in 2019. Being part of the governmental leadership of the house, her responsibilities grew, as did her maturity as a believer and her insight into the Word of God. She started to minister in the house and became a strong pillar in the church family.

When Suhaina approached me with her first book, "What about
the Church?" I was not surprised. I have seen her grow tremen-
dously in the past decade, on every level. She started writing
in church, started her business in church, built friendships in
church, and met her husband in church. Suhaina has experienced a level of spiritual maturity she could have only reached by
being rooted in a local church family. Suhaina might have experienced hurt like so many of us, but she has always persevered
- by God's grace- in trying to understand and be active in the
vehicle on earth (the church), God chose to connect His sons
and daughters together.

In "What about the Church?" you will read about her story,
upbringing, culture, and search for God and faith. What I love
about this book is that she not only shows the relevance of
church based on her experiences but also uses the Word of God
to give us more insight and understanding into why church is
important for any believer. She has a great way of explaining
scripture and keeping us interested in further studying the Word.

Is the church still relevant today or even necessary for believers?
Regardless of your good or bad experiences, I highly recom-
mend reading this well-written piece by Suhaina Benilia-Sophia
and discovering the truth that will undoubtedly boost your spiritual appetite. You will enjoy it, but most of all, you will learn
from it and be inspired by it!

Stefan Lakhichand,
Director Public Transformation
Founder and former pastor of Heaven Designed Life,
Author of "Giving Birth to your Promise" and "Sammy the Superhero."

Preface

Life can take interesting turns. I started at a certain place in my beliefs, and now I'm in a completely different place. It's what happened in between that I want to write about. I wrote this book not to bash those I encountered and certainly not to talk badly about anyone. I want to write about my experience with and in the church. I want to tell you how, despite bad experiences, I still believe in being part of a church community as part of God's plan for people's lives, and I hope to inspire you to do the same.

Introduction

Being a Christian for about 18 years, I can say that I've been in church for a great part of that time. I've had good times and bad times in church. At a certain moment, I was convinced that no matter the mess we as people might have made of the church, the church was, is, and will always be a part of God's plan for His believers.

In this book, I aim to take you on a journey through my story. Not only that, but I also want to show you, with the help of the Word of God, which should be the final authority for every believer, that the church is God's chosen vehicle to bring about His plan for His kingdom.

I hope that when you finish reading this book, you will see the relevance of the church today and find out where you fit in according to God's plan for your life.

Reading Guide for Part 2 of the Book

In this part of the book, we will dig deeper into the Bible. We will look at what the New Testament says about the church. I will use some scriptures that are relevant for each topic, but of course, in your own study, you will discover much more.

In each topic, you will find:

- An introduction and reflection.
- Bible verses: These are verses that are relevant for the church.
- Bold and italic words: For these words, we will look at their original Greek meaning to hopefully get a better understanding of the Bible verse in question.
- Conclusion at the end of every section.

Part 1

My Story

(Religious) Background

I was born on the island of Curaçao, in the Caribbean. I grew up in my grandparents' house, where we lived with my mom, aunts, uncles, and cousins. My mom had me when she was young, so we lived there for a while. I remember the house always being full of people. As a child, I didn't have an opinion about that, but as I grew older, I didn't like being in a busy home all the time. My biological father was not really in the picture, but my stepfather has been beside us since my birth. The first gift I received as a baby was from him. Growing up in a busy household had its advantages; someone was always home after school. We lived in the San Nikolaas neighborhood on the west side of the island.

A day in my childhood went as follows: I would wake up early and shower with cold water *(brrrr)*. I would then put on my school uniform, get my lunch in my schoolbag, and eat something small for breakfast, like cookies and tea. I never missed this in the morning because my grandmother and my mother would only let me leave the house when I had something warm in my belly. After that, I would wait for the school bus and ride on it as I went to school in a different neighborhood, about 15–20 minutes from where I lived.

School started at 7:30 a.m. and was over by 12:30 p.m. I remember that on Mondays, we began the week with the whole school assembled, and on Friday afternoons, we closed off the week by singing the national anthem before starting the weekend. After school, I would wait for the school bus to take me home. Although it was a journey of about 20 minutes, it could take longer to get home if the bus lady dropped off other kids in other areas first.

On the island, eating warm food in the afternoon and something light in the evening is customary. But seeing that the adults in my home worked during the day and got home in the late afternoon, that's when we had dinner. My mother worked at the airport, meaning she worked in shifts. When I would get home from school, she would not be home yet. There was always an aunt or uncle home, and we would always wait for my grandmother to come home. I remember her working on Monday, Wednesday, and Thursday at a house in Sun Valley and Cas Abou on Tuesday and Friday. She worked as a cleaning lady. Monday, Wednesday, and Friday were my favorite days because she would go to Punda and buy us stuff. Thus, I was always excited to wait for her. My grandmother was the responsible adult who cared for us until our parents got home from work. I don't remember much of my grandfather; he died when I was about five. After my grandfather died, my grandmother had to take care of her six children and some grandchildren. Some of my aunts and uncles moved to the Netherlands for a better future. After that, I was the only grandchild living in the house. My afternoons were spent doing homework and watching TV. I learned Spanish from all the TV I watched as a child. I was very good at Spanish at school. I had to learn grammar at school, though. As a young child, I also played outside, especially when my cousins lived there. After they moved, I spent less time playing outside. I was occupied watching TV, playing with Barbie dolls, and reading. When I got older, chores were added to that list. I learned to do chores at a young age. I absolutely hated it at the time, but in retrospect, it gave me a great sense of responsibility.

One thing that I loved about my childhood was my grandmother's cooking. Seeing that she loved cooking and was good at it, she did the cooking in the house. She often took on cooking jobs for parties and funerals in the neighborhood.

I remember that we used to visit the beach most Saturdays, which was around a ten-minute drive away. Our favorite beach was "**Jeremi.**" It was a secluded beach frequented mostly by locals. These were the things I loved during my childhood.

The island's predominant religion is Catholicism, and I was no exception as a typical native-born islander. I was baptised as a baby, received my first communion, and underwent confirmation, all within the Catholic Church. From my earliest memories, my mother and I went to church often, especially during the big holidays. Going to church was a regular part of our lives. As a child, I was well aware of God's existence. A significant part of our culture is intertwined with this belief; however, it is combined with superstitions and cultural customs. Many of our expressions incorporate God. Phrases like "Danki Dios" (thank God), "Ku Dios ke" (God willing), and "Dios mester libra!" (Let it not be so!) are familiar to anyone from Curaçao.

When I reflect on how I encountered God during my childhood, I must say that I was consistently conscious of His existence. Despite the prevailing Catholic faith in our culture and family, there was a period—whose duration I cannot recall—when I attended a different type of church. I'm uncertain of its denomination; looking back now, I believe it might have been a Pentecostal church.

Every Saturday, the church would send a van to pick us up. We would go to a place for "Sunday school," but on Saturdays. We would sing and learn from the Bible. Those were truly fun times.

Apart from that, I attended a Catholic school where the entire school would typically gather for church services either on the first or last Friday of each month. This was convenient, as most schools on the island were within walking distance of a church.

Arriving early often meant having a chance to join the church choir. I wasn't particularly fond of participating, but my teacher during that time oversaw the choir. Being chosen to sing left you no option but to comply.I remember this one time I got to church early, and, of course, I did not want to sing. I saw the teacher standing at the church door searching for kids to pick for that day, and I hid so she could not find me (LOL). I was not up for it that day.

I wanted to live right, though, because my religion emphasized that I pursue this. I also believed that God would punish you if you failed to live right or did something against His commandments, and so it went on. I continued visiting the church regularly. I remember this one time we were in church, although

*Going to church was a regular part
of our lives. As a child, I was well
aware of God's existence.
A significant part of our culture is
intertwined with this belief; however,
it is combined with superstitions and
cultural customs.*

I don't exactly remember how old I was then; I think I was around ten. During the service, the priest said something fascinating, and I felt like I had learned something that day. I remember thinking, *"Church should always be like this. I'm supposed to learn something at church."* After that, I believe I just went through the motions of tradition, attending church regularly and on Christian holidays.

I started going to a Catholic youth group in my early teens. It was very interesting as we discussed the Bible and made what we believed practical. At this youth group, I bought my first Bible (I still have it).

My first and only Bible was in my native language, Papiamentu; it is something I cherish. For most of my childhood, I was hungry for God and His ways, so I enjoyed this youth group I was a part of very much. One highlight of being part of this group was a youth conference that was held. Contrary to most church services I had experienced, this conference was very charismatic, and I had a really good time. Looking in retrospect, knowing what I know now, I think that there were some things that went on at that conference that were unbiblical.

I don't know how I stopped attending those meetings, but, with this background, my view of God and the church was formed.

After I started high school, I believe that I did not go to church as much. I went to a Catholic high school, so we did go to mass occasionally. I remember my physics teacher saying once that he believed in God but didn't believe in the Pope as the head of the church. He even told us that he could get fired from his job by saying that. That was interesting to hear, and it made me curious. I thought, "Why doesn't he agree with that?" I wanted to know more about that, but he couldn't say much concerning it as he was employed at a Catholic school. But to this day, I still remember his remark.

I always believed that God existed, that He was the creator of mankind, and that we ought to worship Him. I don't remember how much I knew about the Bible, though. I know that at some point, I decided that I was going to read the whole Bible (I was and always will be a reader). But that was before I had the one in Papiamentu. My mom had one in Spanish, and I made it my goal to read it from start to finish. It was complicated old Spanish, though. I think I stopped reading at Leviticus.

When I got my Papiamentu Bible, it became easier to read. I read most of the time when I had a nightmare or something like that.

I thought that you should believe in God but, of course, also enjoy life. And I always thought that Christians were a bit too much. There was a lot I did not understand about them, like why they gave money to the church and waited until marriage to have sex. I honestly thought they were weirdos.

As a Catholic, you also have a certain pride; I knew I had that. I thought Catholicism was the right religion, and the others were too fanatical or something like that.

Why did believing in God mean you had to go door to door on Saturdays? Why did you have to wear only long skirts? Why couldn't you have your ears pierced? Why couldn't you enjoy life and believe in God? It did not make sense to me, so I was fine the way I was.

....

Moving to the Netherlands

When the next phase of my life began, I decided to move to the Netherlands to go to college. When I moved here, I was so busy in this new environment that attending church became less of a priority.

My best friend at that time started going to church, and because we had sleepovers on the weekends, I went to church with her. From what I can remember, I enjoyed joining her for church most of the time. I mostly enjoyed the charismatic singing that they had. I also remember joining their youth group for activities like camping at a Pentecostal conference for the weekend, and at another time a youth camp. Those were wonderful experiences. I started getting used to attending church with her, and I wished there was a church like that in my city. I doubted there would be something like that where I lived, but I started searching because I missed it when I was not visiting my friend.

At this time, I was introduced to some online Bible teachers like Joyce Meyer and Creflo Dollar, among others. When I was not visiting my friend and attending church with her, I turned to online teachings and made notes. I was learning a lot. Those who know Joyce Meyers know that you cannot follow her teachings and not be transformed; you will have an attitude change. This encouraged me to look for churches in my city on the internet.

I found a church I thought was fine and started visiting there. It was a big church with about 500 people, if not more. When I started going there, I would leave as soon as the service was over because I didn't know anyone there, and it was a bit scary to stay behind when I didn't know anyone. But I continued to go, and after some time, I started talking to one girl. I think it was during a youth meeting or a regular meeting, and she invited me to a youth gathering. It was very nice to meet someone in that big church. After a while, she invited me to her house for dinner, and I got to spend time with her, her family, and another family visiting them. That was very nice. But after some time, the girl and her family moved from the Netherlands to another country. I'm unsure if I had already gotten to know more people in the church by then, but I know it was very sad to lose someone I had such a good connection with.

In the meantime, I attended more church activities and understood that there was a youth group gathering every Sunday evening, which I started attending.

One of the things I was looking for at this time was people my age to connect with. While I attended those youth meetings, I learned a lot and got to know some amazing people, but still, I was missing some friends my age I had more in common with. I found myself in a difficult situation. I was not born here; I studied, lived in a dorm, and needed some friends nearby who could somehow understand that phase of my life.

However, most of those I met were studying, still living with their parents, and born in the country. When I went to the Sunday services, I learned a lot, but it was a little different from what I saw online. But it stimulated me to read my Bible and grow further in my beliefs. The Sunday services, Bible studies, and church services I visited online were the spiritual food I needed at the time.

Conversion

One day, I was in my room reading the Bible. I read the passage where Jesus was in Gethsemane and asked God the Father if it was possible to let this cup pass Him by. But not His will, but the will of the Father be done. This is something I cannot put into words. I knew at that moment that I was feeling God's love for me. His love went through the worst kind of suffering for me. It was the love I had been looking for all my life. I remember saying to myself, ***"This is real love; this is what I want to belong to."*** At that moment, I accepted Christ into my life. After that, during a church service, there was a call for those who wanted to be baptized. I knew this was my time. Barely knowing anyone, I walked to the front after the service to give myself up to be baptized by immersion. That is one of the things I came to understand—baptism is something that should be your own decision. That day, that decision was made.

The person I talked to asked me, "Have you accepted Jesus as your Lord and Savior?" Without hesitating, I said, "Yes." I can imagine why he had to ask. He had probably never seen me before in the church, and now I'm coming up and saying that I want to be baptized. Anyway, that was a whole experience—a beautiful experience. I started to love God's Word more and more. When in church or watching online, I was always making

This was a challenge because I did not like to walk up to strangers and talk to them, but I felt no one should visit a church and leave unnoticed.

notes. I started helping in the Sunday school classes. After some time, I stopped. At that time, it felt like I was missing a lot of the Sunday meetings because I worked some weekends.

After that, I went to help with the "coffee team." This team helped with serving tea and coffee after the service, and I did that for quite some time. After that, I joined the hospitality team, which was in charge of talking to new people after the service. This was a challenge because I did not like to walk up to strangers and talk to them, but I felt no one should visit a church and leave unnoticed. During this time, I got to know great people. Somehow, I was connecting more with the older people and not so much with those my age. This was something that kept bothering me. I also got involved with the house groups. I was part of one with people of my age and one with mostly older people. It got to a point where I did not want to go to church because I was returning to my apartment alone without having made any meaningful connections. I kept dragging myself to church because I knew it was important to be part of it.

One day, a friend of mine invited me to another church. It was in a city nearby. I hesitated at first, but I decided to try it.

We went together on Sunday, and this was indeed a different experience. I saw different people, and this church had more people coming from the islands. The first thing that got my attention was the music, the praise, and the worship. It was like a party. Almost unbelievable, I thought, *"Is this real?" "Are we still in The Netherlands?"* I did not know it was possible to worship God in this way in the Netherlands. The preaching was good. It was like the teachings I used to look at on the internet. Needless to say,

I was really impressed. I felt at home. After a couple of weeks, I was convinced I wanted to continue attending this church, but I was conflicted. I attended this church in Delft for at least five years. I got baptized there, and I'm not the kind of person who stands up and leaves because there's something better for me somewhere else. I felt that I couldn't just disappear. I needed to let them know that I was not coming back. I informed those responsible, and they wished and prayed for the best for me. I believe this was in 2012.

Since that day, I have not gone anywhere else but to this church. I loved the worship and the Word; it was a modern church. I felt like I was growing a lot when I was there. After a while, I started attending this church by myself. I found myself in the same situation as in the previous church: I didn't know many people. After some time, I started visiting the youth activities and got to know some people. Some people I knew from high school attended the church, so getting to know people was easier, and I kept going.

I had experienced up until that point in these two churches that it took a while to really get connected with people, which was sad. It was because of my determination that I continued going. I could understand someone who would give up because of how big the congregations were and because they didn't connect easily with the people. I persevered at church 2. They also had youth and young adult gatherings, so I started visiting them. The first event I went to was a party. I don't remember the chronological order of how things went, but I started connecting with some people at some point. I believe that the connection happened when I took the Alpha course. We went through the course, and I got to know those attending and those who led the course.

We were always welcome at their home—lovely people who loved God and had a heart to serve people.

After the Alpha course, I totally felt at home at church 2. I told myself I would not run and join whatever team, even though I felt the urge to help. I waited a while before I started helping on the audio/visual team. I was doing the beamer on Sundays, projecting the song lyrics and other visual aids for the Sunday services. I started to get my drive in my Christian life. I had people I was connecting with, a church where I felt fed, and leaders who were an example to follow. It became one of my best church experiences so far.

The services on Sundays were like a party with good food. The praise and worship were great, and the Word was real meat. Nothing I had ever heard before in real life. I could only dream of these kinds of messages; I thought I could only see them online. I was challenged by what I believed. I was challenged to see beyond religion. I was taught about the kingdom of God. I started to understand that we are made for more than living our lives during the week and attending church on Sundays. I realized I had been given gifts that could be used in, and outside of church. Being the introvert I am, I was always drawn to prayer and prayer meetings. At some point, I joined the morning prayer group that prayed before the service started on Sunday morning. I was growing, so I was happy at this place; it started feeling like a family gathering. I made friends there. We would do stuff together after service on Sundays. I was part of the activities going on there—great stuff!

We formed a women's book club, and on Monday evenings, we were trained in prayer. I learned about governmental prayer and understood our authority in Christ. Organized by the youth group, we did a 24-hour praise and worship session. That was a different experience for me and those present. It was here that I can remember receiving my first vision for someone else, and I had to share it in front of everyone, which was the scariest thing. That was the first experience I can remember having with prophecy. I believe that after that day, I started growing and understanding the prophetic world more.

We also started being trained as a prophetic company. Where we would share a prophetic word with the congregation on Sunday morning, this was something that allowed me to grow in faith. All in all, I was enjoying things at this church.

The Shock!

At a certain point, it was time for our annual conference. I remember feeling that something was not okay. First, it was announced that our leaders would take a period of rest. I thought that was normal, but I was surprised because I didn't see that coming. Regardless, I thought they were humans and should have some time off. The conference went on, but it was a bit different—a lot happened during the conference sessions. After the conference, the senior leaders called a meeting for all the church members. There, they announced that, as senior leaders, they had decided to close the church. In the time that passed after the conference and the meeting, I knew something was up, but I never expected this. The church is closing? *What do you mean the church is closing? How can the church close? Where are we going to gather next week? What is going to happen to us now?*

Initially, I was in shock. It was as if the place I had come to call home for the last two years was disappearing. I didn't understand. They also announced that part of the leadership was gathering in The Hague, and another couple was starting a new work in Rotterdam. I couldn't believe what I was hearing. I knew and loved all these people, and now they placed me in a position where I had to choose where I wanted to be. I want to stay here! I don't want to go anywhere!

At that moment, I remember feeling like I was placed in a position to choose between my mom and dad or my aunt and uncle. *How do I make this choice?* It was difficult. After the unbelief passed, I became angry. I thought, *"Okay, I didn't ask for this."* If I'm placed in a position to choose a side, I need to take some time to make the right decision. I knew that something must have happened before a decision as drastic as this one was taken. Something that we were not told. It felt unfair. So, I thought to myself. I will take the next three weeks to hear from God what He wants me to do. I had no idea what to do. However, during the week, I made a choice. I would have said farewell to the church for good if I had not made that choice.

Anyway, I made a choice. So, **church number 3** began—this meant starting again. It was weird having to go to some other place on Sunday. It was weird not seeing the people I was used to seeing every Sunday. *Where were they? Will they come back? Will they go to another church?* Time went by, and I was getting used to the new situation. The weeks passed, and we had no permanent place to gather. I think that in seven months, we gathered in three different locations. I can't say I settled in, as I felt a lot was happening behind the scenes.

This is not the way to treat people. This is not okay. This time I thought, "Alright, this is it." Now I am truly done with the church. I will stay home, read my Bible, and follow God in that way.

Then we reached the start of 2015. From May 2014 until then, the leaders worked together with our old leaders from **church 2**. But in 2015, they decided to stop this. That was like a second bomb exploding. It confirmed a certain feeling I had thateverything was not okay. After this day, it was like we were physically stripped of what we had. We had very little to continue with as a church. About 50% of the members had eloped the following Sunday, which was unpleasant.

At this point, I was done. I talked to God and said to Him, "Your people are crazy; I don't understand what is happening. You can keep your people; I am done with them. This is crazy. This is not the way to treat people. This is not okay." This time I thought, *"Alright, this is it."* Now I am truly done with the church. I will stay home, read my Bible, and follow God in that way. There were enough online churches I could tune into on Sundays. I will not stop following God, but I will no longer be part of any church. I would still get the spiritual food I needed, drama-free. These were my thoughts for about a couple of weeks. Then we had a couple of prayer and fasting meetings in which we sought God for the time ahead of us because we were starting over—again.

My decision or God's decision?

During the second meeting that we had, my decision was final— it was going to be my last time there. I remember we were with about six people, and there were whiteboards in the room so we could share what we had received from God during prayer. In that meeting, God spoke to me and told me, **"You are staying in this house. You are not going anywhere."**

WHAT?!

Are you kidding me, God? I was protesting in every way, but I knew it was Him speaking to me. It was so clear that I couldn't even think about not obeying His voice. I did not understand a thing about what He had in mind. *Why should I stay here?* Everything in me wanted to leave, but His voice…

At that moment, I decided to stay. We were at our third location, an old school building, which was also a temporary one. It was clear to me that I had to be there. Why? I had no idea. So, I stayed. After this, we moved twice again. The fourth place we were at was a community center; we were there for only a couple of weeks. Then we moved to an old school building, which seemed like a more permanent place. Mind you, while we were moving, we didn't have the chance to build the church. Our focus was mainly on finding a place where we could stay for a longer period. So, while we were at this place, we invested in the room we rented and started forming more teams to support the house. We had good times at that place. Then, two significant things happened. I don't remember in what sequence, anyway. First, the senior leaders had been receiving instructions from God that they had to change locations geographically, and doors were opening in another country. In the first part of 2016, they announced they were emigrating and found another couple to continue leading the house. This was yet another change in barely two years. When they announced the couple that was going to take over their responsibilities, I was at peace. They were familiar faces, and I knew them as trustworthy people. The second unbelievable thing that happened that year was our vacating the building because it was bought by some Muslim party planning to make an Islamic school out of it.

I remember that the transition took place in the second half of 2016. Just as I had observed over the previous two years, I understood that whenever a change in leadership occurred, it was common for certain individuals to leave the church. This could be for different reasons, like an affinity for the former leaders. I don't know how it would have been if the new leaders were strangers to me. Anyway, I understood the transition that the former leaders needed to make. They had words spoken over their lives about this. It was part of their destiny. It was time for the next chapter in their lives. When this happened, I had in mind that my trust was in God. I didn't know what He was doing. I didn't know how this leadership transition was going to work out. I didn't know where this transition was going to lead. But one thing I knew for sure, and I remembered what God told me, was to stay, and I would not play with that. I was not going to go my own way. This was God-guided, and it placed me in a position to grow in trust towards God. Do I trust that He is guiding me? Do I trust that this is part of His plan? Or will I take matters into my own hands and do what I think is best for me?

The transition time was October 2016. I did not experience all of it because I was away for a couple of weeks. I missed the official transition service, but when I returned, we were already in a new situation in a different building because we were chased out of the other building. On top of that, some of our equipment got stolen from the old building; thus, we were starting over again.

Going through this all made me think about what the church is. Or what the church really should be.

It took some adjusting, and we needed to figure out everything again. Having different leaders meant that some people stopped coming on Sunday again. We needed to find our way again. How were we going to continue? What was our name going to be? What would our vision be? In other words, there were many questions that needed answers. On this journey, I was very hopeful. I believed that we could establish something great for God with the work of those involved. Going through all this made me think about what the church is. Or what church really should be. Most of us have an idea of *how* we think the church should be. About *what* we think the church should be. But what was God's intention for the church? What is God's intention for the church today? Do we need to visit a church? Or is it enough to believe in God and worship Him at home? If we don't like the church we attend, can we leave and find another church to worship? That is what I would like to find out in the following part of this book.

Part 2

What does the Bible say about the Church?

If I go out on the street and ask those who come by their opinions about the church, I'm sure everyone would have something good or bad to say. But for a believer, the Bible—the Word of God—is the ultimate authority. We might hold personal opinions about the church or have our own experiences within it, but after all is said and done, the Word of God has the final say. Let's look at scriptures about the church and examine the first-century church in the Bible. What conclusions can we draw when we closely examine the Word?

Foundation of the church

When we look in the New Testament, we see in Matthew 16:18 the first mention of the word "church." Jesus asks His disciples who they say He is, and Peter answers that Jesus is the Son of the living God.

Matthew 16:17–18

Jesus answered and said to him, "Blessed are you, Simon Bar-Jonah, for flesh and blood has not revealed this to you, but My Father who is in heaven. 18 And I also say to you that you are Peter, and on *this rock I will build My **church**, and the gates of Hades shall not prevail against it.*

> **Church** - *ecclesia /ek-klay-see-ah/ (Greek)*: Used in secular Greek for an assembly of citizens and in the Septuagint for the congregation of Israel.

The dominant use in the New Testament is to describe anassembly or company of Christians in the following ways:

1. The whole body of Christians.
2. A local church that constitutes a company of Christians gathering for worship, sharing, and teaching.
3. Churches in a district.

Other related terms are "spiritual house," "a chosen race," and "God's people."[1]

On what rock will Jesus build His church? We see this being answered in Ephesians 2:20.

Ephesians 2:19–22

Now, therefore, you are no longer strangers and foreigners, but fellow citizens with the saints and members of the household of God, 20 **having been built on the foundation of the apostles and prophets,** *Jesus Christ Himself being the chief cornerstone, in whom the whole building, being fitted together, grows into a holy temple in the Lord, in whom you also are being built together for a dwelling place of God in the Spirit.*

---

[1] Source: New Spirit Filled Life Bible - Jack W. Hayford, p. 1504

We read in these verses that the church is built as the household of God on the foundation of the apostles and the prophets, with Jesus being the one they are measured by, and that we as believers are being built together—not into physical buildings—into a place where the Spirit of God will dwell.

In the book of Acts, we can read about the first-century church. We see that the disciples were together in one accord, as Jesus instructed prior to His ascension. The word for "with one accord" in Acts 2:1 in Greek is *"homothumadon"* /hom-oth-oo-mad-*on*/, meaning being unanimous, having mutual consent, being in agreement, having group unity, having one mind, and purpose. *Homothumadon* shows harmony leading to action.

At the beginning of the book of Acts, Jesus told the disciples to wait in Jerusalem and wait for the promise of the Father—the Holy Spirit. And that they would receive power when the Holy Spirit came to be His witnesses.

As the story continues, we can see in Acts 2:42 the focus of the first-century church. They continued **steadfastly in the apostles' doctrine and fellowship, in the breaking of bread, and in prayers.**

The word **"steadfast"** means firmly fixed in place, not subject to change, firm in belief, determination, or adherence.

Fellowship is a word that we have been showered with in our Christian circles. It is good for us to know what this word really means. The Greek word for fellowship is *"koinonia"* /koy-nohn-*ee*-ah/, which means sharing, unity, close association, partnership, participation, a society, communion, fellowship, contributory help, and brotherhood. *Koinonia* is a unity brought about by the Holy Spirit. *Koinonia* cements the believers to the Lord Jesus and to each other.

Verse 43 says that fear came upon those gathering and that many wonders and signs were done through the apostles. Seeing that the result of the fear coming upon them was wonders and signs, the word "fear" here means awe and reverence for God. We see that continuing in the apostles' doctrine, fellowship, breaking bread, and prayer brought this.

As we continue, we also see that the Bible says they had all things in common. Being together in this manner, they knew the needs of those gathering and were willing to meet these needs among themselves.

In verse 46, we see that they continued daily in the temple. They ate their food with gladness and simplicity of heart. They praised God and had favor with all the people. In verse 47, the Lord added to the church daily those who were being saved.

Acts 4:32–33

Now the multitude of those who believed were of one heart and one soul; neither did anyone say that any of the things he possessed was his own, but they had all things in common. And with great power the apostles gave witness to the resurrection of the Lord Jesus. And great grace was upon them all.

These verses tell us that the result of the multitude being of one heart and soul was that the apostle gave witness with great power!

As the verses continue, we can read that no one among them was lacking.

This passage in the book of Acts gives us a good view of what the first-century church community was like, what they did, and where their focus was. The first-century church's focus was:

- The apostles' doctrine: the word on which the house/church is built.
- Fellowship: spending time and sharing each other's lives together.
- The breaking of bread: eating and sharing the Word together.
- Prayer: praying together.

Nowadays, we can easily get caught up in the numbers, schedules, and programs regarding church. I believe that at the core of the church, we should still focus on what Acts 2 tells us. It is true that every church has a different vision and is called to a different community, but let's keep going to the Word and reflect on ourselves if we are still on track.

....

The order in the church

We also see that the twelve apostles asked the disciples to choose seven men of good reputation, full of the Holy Spirit and wisdom, to oversee the daily distribution so they could give themselves to prayer and the ministry of the Word (Acts 6:3–4).

It is good to see that order in the church is important. The apostles assigned people to do the practical matters so they could focus on the Word and prayer. It is of utmost importance that we do not portray one task as more important than the other. We must shift our minds to see all tasks in the church as equal. Yes, some carry more responsibility for heavier matters than others, but that doesn't make one more important than the other. The tasks are not the same, but they are equal. It is perhaps common for a small, young church for the visionary to be busy with the practical aspects. It must not remain this way. The leaders must abide by Acts 6 and appoint those who can take care of the practical aspects of the church. Not because the (senior) leaders are more important, but because this will allow them and others to focus on the responsibility they were given by God and their overseer(s).

When we look at 1 Corinthians 14, we see that this chapter tells us a lot about the order in the church. Here we learn that:

- One who speaks a word of prophecy strengthens the whole church.
- The interpretation of tongues will strengthen the church.
- We should be eager to have the gifts that strengthen the whole church.
- If there's no one to interpret tongues, it is more beneficial for the whole church to be silent.
- Women should not take authority over men in the church or cause disruptions in the meetings.

I always wondered what verses 34 and 35 meant. I have heard a lot said about these verses. In various churches, they are used as guidelines not to have women in leadership positions. It always troubled me. Being a woman, I always asked myself what the Apostle Paul meant and how it applies to me today. The following commentary brings a great deal of clarity to the matter.

1 Corinthians 14:34–35

Let your women keep silent in the churches, for they are not permitted to speak; but they are to be submissive, as the law also says. 35 And if they want to learn something, let them ask their own husbands at home; for it is shameful for women to speak in church.

These verses may be interpreted in various ways. The best interpretation is probably to see Paul as not forbidding women to manifest spiritual gifts in the service (1 Corinthians 11:5, Acts 2:18, Acts 21:9). Rather, he prohibits undisciplined discussion that would disturb the service. Also possible is the forbidden speaking along the lines of 1 Timothy 2:11–15, which precludes women from becoming independent doctrinal (apostolic) authorities over men. One other view sees verses 34–35 as Paul's quoting from their letter to him at the beginning of a new paragraph. Proponents of this view then see verse 36 as his rhetorical answer, essentially saying, "What? Men only? Nonsense!"

Perhaps more helpful is noting that the Greek word here for "woman" is also translatable as "wife." Thus, the command may confront the improperly in any age for a wife to domineeringly issue doctrinal commands and enforce authoritative teachings, embarrassing her husband in public. The Bible does not assign rigid social or church roles to men and women, but it places headship and authority in husbands as an abiding principle for this age[2].

Christ, the head of the church

<u>Ephesians 1:22</u>

*And He put all things **under His feet**, and gave Him to be head over all things to the church,*

> **Under His feet** - *hupotasso /hoop-ot-as-so/*: literally, 'to stand under'. The word suggests subordination, obedience, submission, subservience, and subjection.

We must always keep in mind that Christ is the head of the church, not man. Leaders are appointed, and they follow the example of Christ. They should do as Christ did and continuously point us toward the Father.

The church: a place of truth

<u>1 Timothy 3:14–15</u>

These things I write to you, though I hope to come to you shortly; 15 but if I am delayed, I write so that you may know how you ought to conduct yourself in the house of God, which is the church of the living God, the pillar and ground of the truth.

---

[2]   source: New Spirit Filled Life Bible - Jack W. Hayford, p. 1601

The church is the pillar and the ground/foundation of truth. The church ought to be where the truth of God's Word is spoken, where the truth of God's Word is taught, and where the truth of God's Word is lived.

....

The Holy Spirit in the first church

The book of Acts also showed us that great persecution occurred against the first-century church. We must realize that the church is a spiritual entity. The church is the chosen vehicle of God to advance His kingdom. From the very beginning, it has encountered opposition and persecution. I believe that we can expect this to continue at every age and time. It might look different in each part of the world, but it will never change. We must be courageous and know that the church can never be stopped because it is fueled by the Spirit of God. The Spirit that brings life, the Spirit that IS life!

Acts 9:31

*Then the churches throughout all Judea, Galilee, and Samaria had peace and were edified. And walking in the fear of the Lord and in the **comfort** of the Holy Spirit, they were multiplied.*

Here, the Scriptures tell us that there was growth when the churches walked in fear of the Lord and the comfort of the Holy Spirit.

> The Greek word for **comfort** is *paraklesis /par-ak-lay-sis/*, meaning a calling alongside help, comfort, and consolation or encouragement.

The *paraklete* is a strengthening peace that upholds those appealing for assistance. *Paraklesis* can come to us both by the Holy Spirit and by the Scriptures[3].

The comfort, help, encouragement, etc., of the Holy Spirit played a great part in the growth of the church.

The first church of non-Jewish believers

In the Bible, we read how the Word of God spread beyond the Jewish people.

In Acts 11:19–26, we see that the first church consisting of non-Jewish believers was born in the city of Antioch.

Acts 11:19–24

*Now those who were scattered after the persecution that arose over Stephen traveled as far as Phoenicia, Cyprus, and Antioch, preaching the word to no one but the Jews only. But some of them were men from Cyprus and Cyrene, who, when they had come to Antioch, spoke to the Hellenists, preaching the Lord Jesus. And the hand of the Lord was with them, and a great number believed and turned to the Lord. Then news of these things came to the ears of the church in Jerusalem, and they sent out Barnabas to go as far as Antioch. When he came and had seen the grace of God, he was glad, and encouraged them all that with **purpose** of heart they should continue with the Lord. For he was a **good** man, full of the Holy Spirit and of **faith**. And a great many people were added to the Lord.*

---

[3]   Source New Spirit Filled Life Bible - Jack W. Hayford, p. 1508

> **Purpose** - *prothesis /proth-es-is/*: the word suggests a deliberate plan, a proposition, an advance plan, an intention, a design.
> **Good** - *agathos /ag-ath-oss/*: Good, in a physical and moral sense, produces benefits. The word is used for persons, things, acts, conditions, etc.
> **Faith** - *pistis /pis-tis/*: conviction, confidence, trust, belief, reliance, trustworthiness, and persuasion.

In the New Testament setting, pistis is the divinely implanted principle of inward confidence, assurance, trust, and reliance in God and all that He says. The word sometimes denotes the object or content of belief [4].

Acts 11:25–26

Then Barnabas departed for Tarsus to seek Saul. And when he had found him, he brought him to Antioch. So it was that for a whole year they assembled with the church and taught a great many people. And the disciples were first called Christians in Antioch.

In this portion of scripture, we see how the gospel of Jesus Christ was carried to other parts of the ancient world and that a church was formed at that place.

In Acts 13:2–3, we read that as they were praying and fasting, the Holy Spirit revealed to them that Paul and Barnabas needed to be sent.

The Word says that they **ministered** to the Lord.

---

[4]   Source New Spirit Filled Life Bible - Jack W. Hayford, pp. 1563, 1660, 1372

> **ministered** - *leitourgeo /lie-toorg-eh-oh/*: performing religious or charitable acts, fulfilling an office, discharging a function, officiating as a priest, serving God with prayers and fastings.

The Word describes the Aaronic priesthood ministering Levitical services. In Romans 15:27, it is used for meeting the financial needs of the Christians, performing a service to the Lord by doing so. Here, the Christians at Antioch were fulfilling an office and discharging a normal function by ministering to the Lord in fasting and prayer[5].

The church in Antioch was an apostolic church, a sending church. A place where people were trained and sent out with a mission. The church nowadays must reflect this sending aspect. We must understand that it is in the DNA of the church to train and send people to do the work of God. We must also remember to seek God in the decisions we have to make. Let us never make decisions because of pressure, but may we always allow the Holy Spirit to guide us to make the right choices at the right time.

....

The price that was paid for the church

We are all familiar with buying something. In our economy, we know that there are cheap and expensive products. We are careful with a product that costs a lot of money. How does this apply to the church? God found that there was no earthly currency that was fit. Let's look at the verse below.

---

[5] Source New Spirit Filled Life Bible - Jack W. Hayford, p. 1515

We should repent for taking the church for granted. We should repent of regarding the church as not important or relevant.

"So guard yourselves and God's people. Feed and shepherd God's flock—his church, purchased with his own blood—over which the Holy Spirit has appointed you as leaders.

We should aim for harmony in the church and build each other up. It was not a cheap price that was paid for the church, but rather the ultimate price. The Father found it fitting that the price to pay for the church was the blood of Jesus Christ. The price paid for the church was THE BLOOD OF JESUS CHRIST! Do you realize this? How important do you think this makes the church?

We should repent for taking the church for granted. We should repent of regarding the church as not important or relevant.

If this was the price that was paid, we must never lose hope in the church. We should respect the church. We should do our best for the welfare of the church. We should always find our way back to the church. We must continue to believe in the church. It was worth the blood of Christ.

....

Attitude in the church

When the Bible describes certain communities of believers, it also describes how we should relate to one another and how we should conduct ourselves. Let us look at some of these verses. I hope these inspire us to look further into how our attitudes in the church **should and should not be**.

Harmony

So then, let us aim for harmony in the church and try to build each other up.

This must be one of the things we aim for in the church: harmony and building each other up. It is easier said than done. We must remember that the only thing that happens automatically is chaos, which is also true in the church. It is easy to take offense. It is easy to dwell on something that might only be a misunderstanding. It is easy to assume. It is easy to gossip. But with the Holy Spirit, let us try to live by this verse.

Romans 12:10–13

*Be kindly affectionate to one another with **brotherly love**, in honor giving preference to one another; not lagging in diligence, **fervent** in spirit, serving the Lord; rejoicing in hope, **patient** in tribulation, continuing steadfastly in prayer; distributing to the needs of the saints, given to hospitality.*

Brotherly love -
philadelphia /fil-ad-el-fee-ah/:
from phileo, 'to love', and
adelphos, 'brother'.

The word denotes the love of brothers and fraternal affection. The New Testament describes the love Christians have for other Christians.

Fervent - zeo /dzeh-oh/:
living fervor, fiery hot, full of
burning zeal.

Fervent is the opposite of dignified, cold, and unemotional. In a Christian context it signifies a high spiritual temperature inflamed by the Holy Spirit.

This is not passive resignation to fate and mere patience but the active, energetic resistance to defeat that allows calm and brave endurance[6].

These verses beautifully describe the attitude we must have toward one another, although it is easier said than done. But remember, nothing the Bible tells us to do is something we can do in our strength. Even the words we read were written under the inspiration of the Holy Spirit. Most certainly, the execution thereof must be, too!

When we find it hard to love our fellow brothers and sisters, we must cry out to the Father for strength—for the Holy Spirit to help us do that which is difficult, hard, or impossible.

Beware of divisions

Wherever there are people, you'll find the possibility of everyone going their own way. This should certainly not be the case in a church. As the verse below says, we should make an effort to stay united.

1 Corinthians 1:10 (NLT)

I appeal to you, dear brothers and sisters, by the authority of our Lord Jesus Christ, to live in harmony with each other. Let there be no divisions in the church. Rather, be of one mind, united in thought and purpose.

---

[6]   Source New Spirit Filled Life Bible - Jack W. Hayford, pp. 1745, 1526, 1335

1 Corinthians 1:10 (NKJV)

*Now I plead with you, brethren, by the name of our Lord Jesus Christ, that you all speak the same thing, and that there be no divisions among you, but that you be **perfectly joined together** in the same mind and in the same judgment.*

> **Perfectly joined together** in this verse is the word *katartizo /kat-ar-tid-zoe) meaning*: to arrange, set in order, equip, adjust, complete what is lacking, make fully ready, repair, prepare.

Example: It is used for the disciples' mending their nets and for restoring a fallen brother.[7]

When we choose to be part of a church, it should not be a decision we make lightly. We must realize that we are not only joining a place to gather on Sunday. We must be aware that we are joining a place with a certain vision. A place where we will grow. A place where we will be challenged. A place where we will be formed to be perfectly joined together.

There ought not to be divisions between us (as we celebrate the Lord's Supper).

1 Corinthians 11:17–19 (NLT)

But in the following instructions, I cannot praise you. For it sounds as if more harm than good is done when you meet together. 18 First, I hear that there are divisions among you when you meet as a church, and to some extent I believe it. 19 But, of course, there must be divisions among you so that you who have God's approval will be recognized!

---

[7] Source New Spirit Filled Life Bible - Jack W. Hayford, p. 1741

<u>1 Corinthians 11:17–19 (NKJV)</u>

*Now in giving these instructions I do not praise you, since you come together not for the better but for the worse. 18 For first of all, when you come together as a church, I hear that there are divisions among you, and in part I believe it. 19 For there must also be **factions** among you, that those who are approved may be **recognized** among you.*

> **Factions/Divisions/heresies** - *hairheseis /hahee-res-is/*: the word originally denoted making a choice or having an opinion.

Progressing to having a preference because of an opinion or a sentiment, it easily slipped into a mode of disunity, choosing sides, having a diversity of belief, creating dissension, and substituting self-willed opinions for submission to the truth. The dominant use in the New Testament is to signify sects, people professing opinions independent of the truth[8].

> **Recognized** - *phaneros /fan-er-oss/*: conspicuous, apparent, manifest, visible, evident, plain, clear, open to sight.

The very nature of the word suggests visibility that gives the observer an ability to define what is seen instantly[9].

We must realize that we WILL have our own opinions, but our opinions should never be placed above the truth. We should always allow the truth of the Word to guide us to a solution.

---

[8] Source: New Spirit Filled Life Bible - Jack W. Hayford, p. 1776
[9] Source: New Spirit Filled Life Bible - Jack W. Hayford, p. 1595

Immorality

*It is actually reported that there is **sexual immorality** among you, and such sexual immorality as is not even named among the Gentiles—that a man has his father's wife! And you are puffed up, and have not rather mourned, that he who has done this deed might be taken away from among you. For I indeed, as absent in body but present in spirit, have already judged (as though I were present) him who has so done this deed.*

We should not condone sexual immorality in the church or overlook it because of the gifts of the people. The church should be a place where those who struggle in this area can find restoration. We must be equipped to help and restore.

> The word used for **sexual immorality** is the Greek word *porneia / por-ni-ah/*, which means illicit sexual intercourse, including prostitution, whoredom, incest, licentiousness, adultery, and habitual immorality.

(Ex.) The word describes both physical immorality and spiritual, signifying idolatry[10].

The explanation above shows that the word for immorality in the verse above also speaks of idolatry. Yet I believe there is much more judgment in the church toward sexual immorality than idolatry, even though both come from the same root word.

---

[10] Source: New Spirit Filled Life Bible - Jack W. Hayford, p. 1318

1 Corinthians 5:12 tells us that we are responsible for judging (to administer corrective discipline to) those who sin in the church.

Firstly, we must have a good understanding of the word "judge," not to make people feel bad about themselves and their behavior but to address them in a way that corrects them. As the global church, I believe we have a much better job to do here. How many people leave and stay away from the church because they are judged by it?

If one has something against a brother or sister that concerns the spiritual life, we ought to consult those in the church who are wise (according to 1 Corinthians 6) to address the situation.

Ephesians 5:3–4 (NKJV)

But fornication and all uncleanness or covetousness, let it not even be named among you, as is fitting for saints; 4 neither filthiness, nor foolish talking, nor coarse jesting, which are not fitting, but rather giving of thanks.

Ephesians 5:3–4 (NLT)

Let there be no sexual immorality, impurity, or greed among you. Such sins have no place among God's people. 4 Obscene stories, foolish talk, and coarse jokes—these are not for you. Instead, let there be thankfulness to God.

These verses show us the behavior that should not be among believers, and they challenge us to be thankful in every circumstance. The moment we are tempted to do one of the abovementioned things, I believe that finding something to thank God for is the way out.

I will not claim that this is an exhaustive list, but these verses give us a good direction on how our attitude should be.

The core of coming together

Many churches in this modern time start in homes, which is not new to our times. In the New Testament, we see many people meeting in each other's homes. Let's look at some examples.

Romans 16:5

Also, give my greetings to the church that meets in their home. Greet my dear friend Epenetus. He was the first person from the province of Asia to become a follower of Christ.

1 Corinthians 16:19

The churches of Asia greet you. Aquila and Priscilla greet you heartily in the Lord, with the church that is in their house.

In the time of the early church, it was common for believers to meet at their homes. However, in our day and age, having a big church and a big building is the measure by which success is defined. We must revisit the beginnings. Having a big church in terms of the number of people is not wrong. But we must remember that it was not the focus of the early church. The focus of the early church was on the well-being and spiritual growth of every believer. Looking at the early church, we will realize that the core was the meeting in homes, where lives could be shared.

Our identity as believers

The whole Bible speaks about our identity in Christ. Let's look at some of these verses that clearly describe who we are in Him.

1 Corinthians 1:2 (NKJV)

*To the church of God which is at Corinth, to those who are **sanctified** in Christ Jesus, called to be **saints**, with all who in every place call on the name of Jesus Christ our Lord, both theirs and ours.*

> **Sanctified** - *hagiadzo /hag-ee-ad-zoe/*: to hallow, set apart, separate, sanctify, make holy. Hagiadzo, as a state of holiness, is the opposite of koinon, common or unclean.

In the OT, things, places, and ceremonies were named hagiadzo. In the New Testament, the word describes a manifestation of life produced by the indwelling Holy Spirit. Because His Father set Him apart, Jesus is appropriately called the Holy One of God[11].

> **Saints** - *hagios /hag-ee-oss/*: sacred, pure, blameless, consecrated, separated, properly revered, worthy of veneration, Godlikeness, God's innermost nature, set apart for God, reserved for God and His service

Since nothing polluted could be *hagios*, purity becomes a big part of *hagios*. A holy God calls for a holy people[12].

---

[11] Source: New Spirit Filled Life Bible - Jack W. Hayford, p. 1463
[12] Source: New Spirit Filled Life Bible - Jack W. Hayford, p. 1502

I am writing to God's church in Corinth, to you who have been called by God to be his own holy people. He made you holy by means of Christ Jesus, just as he did for all people everywhere who call on the name of our Lord Jesus Christ, their Lord and ours.

Those belonging to the church have been called by God Himself to be His people. When we decide to accept God and join a church, we think that it is a decision we made, but it was God who chose us and took us up into His family. We must always be aware that we don't belong to ourselves; we must remember that He called us. And if He called us to be His people, it was with a purpose.

Gifts given to the church

1 Corinthians 12:28 tells us about the gifts that God has given to the church.

*And God has appointed these in the church: first **apostles**, second **prophets**, third teachers, after that miracles, then gifts of healings, helps, administrations, varieties of tongues. (NKJV)*

> **Apostles** - *apostolos /ap-os-tol-oss/:* a special messenger, a delegate, one commissioned for a particular task or role, one who is sent forth with a message.

In the New Testament, the word denotes both the original twelve disciples and prominent leaders outside the Twelve. Marving Vincent records three features of an apostle:

1. One who has had a visible encounter with the resurrected Christ.
2. One who plants churches.
3. One who functions in the ministry with signs, wonders, and miracles[13].

> **Prophet** - *prophetes /prof-ay-tace/*: a prophet is primarily a forth-teller, one who speaks forth a divine message that can at times include foretelling future events.

Among the Greeks, the prophet was the interpreter of the divine will, and this idea is dominant in biblical usage. Prophets are therefore specially endowed with insights into the counsels of the Lord and serve as His spokesman. Prophecy is a gift of the Holy Spirit, which the New Testament encourages believers to exercise, although at a level different from those with the prophetic office[14].

We must realize that those apostles, prophets, etc., are gifts given by God. We must not cultivate a sense of entitlement when it comes to the leaders of the church. What do I mean by that? I mean that we must know that although they are placed in the church to lead us, we don't own them. I mean that we must realize that our leaders are humans, too. They need everything we need, too. It doesn't mean that because they are set as leaders in the church, they owe us something. We ought to aim to make the work pleasant and easy for them. Indeed, the apostles, prophets, and teachers are there for us, but let us think of them. Let

---

[13] Source: New Spirit Filled Life Bible - Jack W. Hayford, p. 1598
[14] Source: New Spirit Filled Life Bible - Jack W. Hayford, p. 1291

*These people are given as a gift to
the church for a reason: to fulfill
a specific role. To do work. We
must know that being an apostle
or teacher is not a title to add
to our name as a degree. It is a
responsibility to carry in equipping
the house of God.*

us think about their family and their work outside of the church. Let us think about a way we can help them. Let us not take them for granted. Let us not see them as people we can only benefit from.

These people are given as a gift to the church for a reason: to fulfill a specific role. To do work. We must know that being an apostle or teacher is not a title to add to our name as a degree. It is a responsibility to carry in equipping the house of God.

In Ephesians 3, Paul talks about the mystery now revealed, that the Gentiles are also fellow heirs in the body of Christ. Verse 10 tells us that through the church, the **manifold** wisdom of God is to be made known to the principalities and powers in the heavenly places.

As a God of variety, He is still entering the human arena displaying many-sided, multicolored, and much-variegated wisdom to His people and through His people[15].

God chose the church to manifest the many expressions of His wisdom.

....

Christ and His church

We know there is a mystery in the relationship between Christ and His church. Let's read Ephesians 5:22–33 and focus on some keywords in these passages.

---

[15] Source: New Spirit Filled Life Bible - Jack W. Hayford, p. 1649

Ephesians 5:22–23

*Wives, submit to your own husbands, as to the Lord. For the husband is head of the wife, as also Christ is head of the church; and He is the **Savior** of the body.*

> **Savior** - *soter /so-tare/*: From the same root as sodzo, 'to save, and soteria, 'salvation'.

The word designates a deliverer, preserver, savior, benefactor, and rescuer. It is used to describe both God the Father and Jesus the Son[16].

Ephesians 5:24–25

*Therefore, just as the church is subject to Christ, so let the wives be to their own husbands in everything. Husbands, love your wives, just as **Christ** also loved the church and gave Himself for her.*

> **Christ** - *Christos /Khris-toss/*: the Anointed One.

The word comes from the verb *chrio*, 'to anoint', referring to the consecration rites of a priest or king. *Christos* translates the Hebrew *Mashiyach*, 'Messiah'. Unfortunately, the transliteration of *Christos* onto English, resulting in the word 'Christ', deprives the word of much of its meaning. It would be better to translate *Christos* in every instance as 'the Anointed One' or 'the Messiah', denoting a *title*. 'Jesus Christ' actually means Jesus the Messiah, or Jesus the Anointed One, emphasizing the fact that the man,

---

[16] Source: New Spirit Filled Life Bible - Jack W. Hayford, p. 1450

Jesus, was God's Anointed One, the promised Messiah[17].

Ephesians 5:26–31

that He might sanctify and cleanse her with the washing of water by the word, that He might present her to Himself a glorious church, not having spot or wrinkle or any such thing, but that she should be holy and without blemish. So, husbands ought to love their own wives as their own bodies; he who loves his wife loves himself. For no one ever hated his own flesh, but nourishes and cherishes it, just as the Lord does the church. For we are members of His body, of His flesh and of His bones. "For this reason, a man shall leave his father and mother and be __joined__ to his wife, and the two shall become one flesh."

> **Joined** - *proskollao /pros-kol-lah-oh/:* to glue or cement together, stick to, adhere to, join firmly.

The word in the New Testament primarily describes the union of husband and wife. The addition of *pros* to *kollao* intensifies the relationship between husband and wife. *Proskollao* includes faithfulness, loyalty, and permanency in relationships[18].

Ephesians 5:32-33

This is a great mystery, but I speak concerning Christ and the church. Nevertheless let each one of you in particular so love his own wife as himself, and let the wife see that she respects her husband.

---

[17] Source: New Spirit Filled Life Bible - Jack W. Hayford, p. 1716
[18] Source: New Spirit Filled Life Bible - Jack W. Hayford, p. 1368

These verses describe the relationship between Christ and the church, which is the same instruction for the relationship between husband and wife. According to these verses:

- Christ is the head of the church. I believe the church mentioned here is the church worldwide. Christ, as the head, is the one who directs the church. What does this look like? This happens through the leaders He has placed in the local houses. Leaders are chosen and confirmed by the Holy Spirit and by seasoned people/leaders. These leaders are responsible for directing the house in the direction revealed through the Holy Spirit.
- The church is subject to Christ. The church stands under Christ, under the authority of Christ. It's not that Christ goes where the church goes, but the other way around. Being under the authority of Christ means following the order that God has set in place.
- Christ's love led Him to die for the church.
- His word cleanses and sets the church apart.
- Christ nourishes and cherishes the church.
- Being part of the church makes us part of His body, His flesh, and His bones.

Reading these verses, it is unmistakable that the church was not an afterthought of God but part of His plan all along—that it is and will be part of His plan. In these verses, we read of the love Christ had and has for His church. Who are we now to think and say that the church is unimportant? If Christ nourishes and cherishes the church, we should do the same. After all, we are being formed to be more like Christ.

....

Some practical instructions

1 Timothy 5:16 instructs that if there's a family member who can take care of their relatives (those who need help), they are to do so. In that way, the church can focus on the widows who depend on it for help.

James 5:14 gives instructions for the sick.

*Is anyone among you sick? Let him call for the elders of the church, and let them **pray** over him, anointing him with oil in the name of the Lord.*

> **Pray** - *proseuchomai /pros-yoo-khom-ahee/*: the word is progressive. Starting with the noun, euche, which is a prayer to God that also includes making a vow, the word expands to the verb euchomai, a special term describing an invocation, request, or entreaty. Adding pros, 'in the direction of' (God), proseuchomai becomes the most frequent word for prayer.

Source[19]

In the Bible, we find other words that relate to the church. Let's look at these words and how they are connected to the church.

....

House of God

The church is also called the House of God. When we speak of a house, we also unmistakably speak of a family. God's intention was and is that the church should be a family. We find that the

---

[19] Source: New Spirit Filled Life Bible - Jack W. Hayford, p. 1300

dynamics are different from those of a random club or social gathering. In a family, we find parents and children. We find those with the responsibility to raise and educate and those with the responsibility to be educated and contribute to the success of the house.

Do we see ourselves as children who need to grow and contribute to the well-being of the house?

Let's look at some scriptures.

Ephesians 2:19

*Now, therefore, you are no longer strangers and **foreigners**, but fellow citizens with the saints and members of the household of God...*

> **Foreigners** - *paroikos /par-oy-koss/*: from para, 'beside', and oikeo, 'to dwell'; hence, 'dwelling near'.

The word came to denote an alien who dwells as a sojourner in a land without the right of citizenship. The word describes Abraham and Moses as sojourners in a land not their own (Acts 7:6, 29). The Christian who is traveling through this world as an alien whose citizenship and ultimate residence are in heaven (1 Peter 2:11)[20].

As Gentiles, we are no longer strangers; we are members of the household of God. Members of a household have rights but also duties. If we look at a natural household, in the ideal situation, we will see parents who take care of their children. These

---

[20] Source: New Spirit Filled Life Bible - Jack W. Hayford, p. 1648

children grow up and start to contribute to the household according to what is appropriate for their age and ability. Finally, they become adults and leave their parental homes to lead responsible lives in society. In the church, it's the same: young believers should receive proper nurturing and education to grow spiritually and to be able to contribute to the well-being of the church. And when the time is right, they should be sent out to continue to expand the kingdom of God.

We should say goodbye to endlessly being fed in a church and never contributing.

1 Timothy 3:14–15

These things I write to you, though I hope to come to you shortly; 15 but if I am delayed, I write so that you may know how you ought to conduct yourself in the house of God, which is the church of the living God, the pillar and ground of the truth.

Hebrews 10:21

Christ rules over God's house.

1 Peter 2:5

you also, as living stones, are being built up a spiritual house, a holy priesthood, to offer up spiritual sacrifices acceptable to God through Jesus Christ.

We, as people, are being built up as the spiritual house of God.

Galatians 6:10

*Therefore, as we have opportunity, **let** us do good to all, especially to those who are of the household of faith.*

> **Let** - *ergazomai /er-gad-zom-ahee/:* to work, be busy, accomplish
> something, carry on a trade, produce things, be engaged in, toil,
> perform, to do business. Ergazomai is the opposite of idleness,
> laziness, or inactivity.

Source[21]

We should put effort into doing good to all we come in
contact with.

The body of Christ

The church is also called the body of Christ. This comparison
is fascinating to me because we have an example of the natural
body we can refer to. Let's look at the scriptures.

Romans 12:4–5

*For as we have many members in one body, but all the members do not
have the same function, so we, by being many are one body in Christ,
and individually members of one another.*

We need to realize that we are not an island as a local church.
The church worldwide forms the body of Christ, meaning each
church is a part of the body. We should not think that our house
is the body and that other churches are less important. I believe
that Jesus' aim is for His body to function properly. For that to
become a reality, all the different parts should know their function or role and where they fit in the body. When each church

---

[21] Source: New Spirit Filled Life Bible - Jack W. Hayford, p. 1448

knows what they are contributing to the body, they can focus on that, not comparison or competition with other churches.

1 Corinthians 12:12–13

*For as the body is one and has many members, but all the members of that one body, being many, are one body, so also is Christ. For by one Spirit we were all baptized into one body—whether Jews or Greeks, whether slaves or **free**—and have all been made to drink into one Spirit.*

> **Free** - *eleutheros /el-yoo-ther-oss/:* freeborn, exempt from a legal obligation, unconstrained. It is the opposite of being enslaved.

The word is derived from the verb *eleuthomai*, 'to come, go', thus describing the freedom to go where one chooses[22].

We need to realize that the Spirit baptizes us into one body; it makes us one. So, we can't decide that we are not related to one another; we can't decide to leave the church at large and do our own thing, as they say.

1 Corinthians 12:14–23

For in fact the body is not one member but many. If the foot should say, "Because I am not a hand, I am not of the body," is it therefore not of the body? And if the ear should say, "Because I am not an eye, I am not of the body," is it therefore not of the body? If the whole body were an eye, where would be the hearing? If the whole were hearing, where would be the smelling? But now God has set the members, each one of them, in the body just as He pleased. And if

---

[22] Source: New Spirit Filled Life Bible - Jack W. Hayford, p. 1826

*they were all one member, where would the body be? But now indeed there are many members, yet one body. And the eye cannot say to the hand, "I have no need of you"; nor again the head to the feet, "I have no need of you." No, much rather, those members of the body which seem to be weaker are necessary. And those members of the body which we think to be less honorable, on these we bestow **greater** honor; and our unpresentable parts have greater modesty…*

Greater - *perissos /per-is-soss/:* superabundance, excessive, overflowing, surplus, over and above, more than enough, profuse, extraordinary, above the ordinary, more than sufficient.

I ask you to go back and read verse 18. God has placed every church just as He pleased, even the ones (church/congregation) we might not understand. We must be reminded that we are there to work together as a well-functioning body. We might not understand everything, but let us remember that we all see in part. That we know something does not mean that we know everything there is to know, and what we don't know, we don't know.

1 Corinthians 12:24–31

but our presentable parts have no need. But God composed the body, having given greater honor to that part which lacks it, that there should be no schism in the body, but that the members should have the same care for one another. And if one member suffers, all the members suffer with it; or if one member is honored, all the members rejoice with it. Now you are the body of Christ, and members individually. And God has appointed these in the church: first apostles, second prophets, third teachers, after that miracles, then gifts of healings, helps, administrations, *varieties of tongues. Are all apostles? Are all prophets? Are all teachers? Are all workers of miracles? Do all have gifts of healings? Do all speak with tongues? Do all interpret? But earnestly **desire** the best **gifts**. And yet I show you a **more excellent** way.*

> **Desire** - *zeloo /dzay-low-o/*: to be zealous for, to burn with desire, to pursue ardently, to desire eagerly or intensely. Negatively, the word is associated with strong envy and jealousy.

> **Gifts** - *charisma /khar-is-mah/*: related to other words derived from the root char. Chara is joy, cheerfulness, and delight. Charis is grace, goodwill, and undeserved favor.

Charism is a gift of grace, a free gift, divine gratuity, spiritual endowment, and miraculous faculty. It is especially used to designate the gifts of the Spirit. In modern usage, a 'charismatic' signifies one who either has one or more of these gifts functioning in his life or believes these gifts are for today's church[23].

> **More excellent** - *huperbole /hoop-er-bol-ay/*: from huper, 'beyond' and ballo, 'to throw'; hence, a throwing beyond. The primary idea is that of excellence, superiority, excess, and preeminence.

Ephesians 1:22–23

And He put all things under His feet, and gave Him to be head over all things to the church, which is His body, the fullness of Him who fills all in all.

---

[23] Source: New Spirit Filled Life Bible - Jack W. Hayford, pp. 1599, 1580, 1614

Let us stand still for a moment and consider what this verse says. Jesus puts ALL things UNDER His feet. With the church being His body, this means that ALL things are under the church, which is the fullness of Jesus.

<u>Ephesians 4:4–6</u>

*There is one body and one Spirit, just as you were called in one **hope** of your calling; one Lord, one faith, one **baptism**; one God and Father of all, who is above all, and through all, and in you all.*

> **Hope** - *elpis /el-peece/*: not in the sense of an optimistic outlook or wishful thinking without any foundation, but in the sense of confident expectation based on solid certainty.

Biblical hope rests on God's promises, particularly those pertaining to Christ's return. So certain is the future of the redeemed that the New Testament sometimes speaks of future events in the past tense, as though they were already accomplished. Hope is never inferior to faith but is an extension of faith. Faith is the present possession of grace; hope is confidence in grace's future accomplishment[24].

> **Baptism** - *baptisma /bap-tis-mah/*: from the verb baptizo, to dip, immerse. Baptisma emphasizes the result of the act rather than the act itself.

In Christian baptism, the emphasis is on the baptized person's identification with Christ in death, burial, and resurrection. The

---

[24] Source: New Spirit Filled Life Bible - Jack W. Hayford, p. 1684

word describes the experience of a convert from initial acceptance of Christ to initiation into the Christian community[25].

Often, it might seem that we are in the business of us versus them in the church. We must be constantly reminded that there is one God and one Spirit that unites us all.

Ephesians 4:11–12

*And He Himself gave some to be apostles, some prophets, some evangelists, and some **pastors** and teachers, for the **equipping** of the saints for the work of ministry, for the edifying of the body of Christ,*

> **Pastors** - *poimen /poy-mane/*: a herdsman, sheepherder; one who tends, leads, guides, cherishes, feeds, and protects a flock.

The New Testament uses the word *poimen* for a Christian pastor to whose care and leadership others will commit themselves. The term is applied metaphorically to Christ[26].

> **Equipping** - *katartismos /kat-ar-tis-moss/*: a making fit, preparing, training, perfecting, making fully qualified for service.

In classical Greek, the word *katartismos* is used for setting a bone during surgery. For instance, a great physician makes all the necessary adjustments so the church will not be 'out of joint'[27].

---

[25] Source: New Spirit Filled Life Bible - Jack W. Hayford, p. 1330
[26] Source: New Spirit Filled Life Bible - Jack W. Hayford, p. 1461
[27] Source: New Spirit Filled Life Bible - Jack W. Hayford, p. 1651

Jesus gave these gifts to the church to equip the saints, edify the body, and bring them to full maturity in Christ. When we look at these, they are not titles but roles that carry responsibility. Someone cannot be either of these and not be doing the work of equipping and edifying the church.

When we look at the definition of the word "equipping," we must realize that part of it must be painful—seeing that one of the definitions comes from "setting a bone during surgery." So, it must not surprise or offend us when what we are taught hurts a little.

Ephesians 4:15–16

*But, speaking the truth in love, may grow up in all things into Him who is the head—Christ— 16 from whom the whole body, joined and knit together by what every joint supplies, according to the effective **working** by which every part does its share, causes growth of the body for the edifying of itself in love.*

The church at large consists of different parts worldwide, and every part needs to contribute for the body to grow. The church needs to grow into the fullness of Christ. We need to aspire to become mature in Him. But this growth happens correctly when it happens in love.

> **Working** - *energeia /en-erg-eye-ah/*: working, action, operative power. The English word energy comes from this word.

Energeia usually describes the working[28] of God but is used for Satan's empowering 'the lawless one' (2 Thessalonians 2:9).

---

[28] Source: New Spirit Filled Life Bible - Jack W. Hayford, p. 1673

Ephesians 5:23

For the husband is head of the wife, as also Christ is head of the church; and He is the Savior of the body.

Christ is the head and the Savior of the church.

Ephesians 5:29–30

For no one ever hated his own flesh, but nourishes and cherishes it, just as the Lord does the church. For we are members of His body, of His flesh and of His bones.

The church is nourished and cherished by Jesus; it should also be cherished and nourished by us.

Colossians 1:18

And He is the head of the body, the church, who is the beginning, the firstborn from the dead, that in all things He may have the preeminence.

Colossians 1:24 (NKJV)

*I now rejoice in my sufferings for you, and fill up in my flesh what is lacking in the **afflictions** of Christ, for the sake of His body, which is the church,*

Afflictions/tribulation - *thlipsis /thlip-sis/:* pressure, oppression, stress, anguish, tribulation, adversity, affliction, crushing, squashing, squeezing, distress.

Imagine placing your hand on a stack of loose items and manually compressing them. That is *thlipsis,* putting a lot of pressure on that which is free and unfettered. *Thlipsis* is like spiritual bench-pressing. The word is used for crushing grapes or olives in a press[29].

Colossians 1:24 (NLT)

I am glad when I suffer for you in my body, for I am participating in the sufferings of Christ that continue for his body, the church.

Like Paul is saying that he rejoices in his sufferings for the church, I believe that the same is true for leaders today. I believe that with leadership comes a certain level of suffering. For some reason, we believe in the glamour of being a leader. But I believe that godly leadership carries a level of suffering. Both leaders and church members are being formed into maturity, so in some instances, that is painful.

Colossians 2:18–19 (NKJV)

*Let no one cheat you of your reward, taking delight in false **humility** and worship of angels, intruding into those things which he has not seen, vainly puffed up by his fleshly mind, 19 and not holding fast to the Head, from whom all the body, **nourished** and knit together by joints and ligaments, grows with the increase that is from God.*

> **Humility** - *tapeinophrosune /tap-eye-nof-ros-oo-nay/*: modesty, lowliness, humble-mindedness, a sense of moral insignificance, and a humble attitude of unselfish concern for the welfare of others. It is a total absence of arrogance, conceit, and haughtiness.

The word is a combination of *tapeinos*, 'humble', and *phren*,

---

[29] Source: New Spirit Filled Life Bible - Jack W. Hayford, p. 1474

'mind'. The word was unknown in classical non-biblical Greek. Only by abstaining from self-aggrandizement can members of the Christian community maintain unity and harmony[30].

> **Nourished/supplies** - *epichoregeo /ep-ee-khor-ayg-eh-oh/*: a combination of epi, intensive, and choregeo, 'to defray the expenses of a chorus'.

The word thus means to supply fully or abundantly, generously provide what is needed, to cover the costs completely. It is used with the strong connotation of great and free generosity[31].

Colossians 2:18–19 (NLT)

Don't let anyone condemn you by insisting on pious self-denial or the worship of angels, saying they have had visions about these things. Their sinful minds have made them proud, and they are not connected to Christ, the head of the body. For he holds the whole body together with its joints and ligaments, and it grows as God nourishes it.

The body of Christ is nourished by what God supplies. Looking at the definition of the word nourished, we can understand that God has supplied and does supply wholly and abundantly what is needed for the body of Christ to grow.

Colossians 3:15

*And let the **peace** of God rule in your hearts, to which also you were called in one body; and be thankful.*

---

[30] Source: New Spirit Filled Life Bible - Jack W. Hayford, p. 1529
[31] Source: New Spirit Filled Life Bible - Jack W. Hayford, p. 1388

Jesus puts ALL things UNDER His feet. With the church being His body, this means that ALL things are under the church, which is the fullness of Jesus.

Eirene includes harmonious relationships between God and men, men and men, nations and families. Jesus, as the Prince of Peace, gives peace to those who call upon Him for personal salvation[32].

We were called into one body through the peace of God. As the church, we should aim to be at peace and united with each other, not emphasizing our differences.

When we look at a natural body, we know that it should function as one. If one part of the body could function independently, it would be shocking because that's not how it's supposed to be. We should also look at the global church in this way, knowing that, as a local church, we are not the body, but we are part of the body of Christ, and we need each other to fulfill the purpose of the body directed by the head, who is Christ.

....

The saints

In the letters to the churches, we see that the believers were called "saints." I'm sure that in church language, you must have heard this term. However, to be called saints or address other believers as saints, we must know what the Word says about the saints. Let's take a look.

---

[32] Source: New Spirit Filled Life Bible - Jack W. Hayford, p. 1388

Acts 9:13

Then Ananias answered, "Lord, I have heard from many about this man, how much harm he has done to Your saints in Jerusalem.

Here, we see that the believers in Jerusalem are addressed as saints.

Acts 9:32

Now it came to pass, as Peter went through all parts of the country, that he also came down to the saints who dwelt in Lydda.

Acts 9:41

Then he gave her his hand and lifted her up; and when he had called the saints and widows, he presented her alive.

Romans 1:7

To all who are in Rome, beloved of God, called to be saints: Grace to you and peace from God our Father and the Lord Jesus Christ.

Romans 8:27

*Now He who searches the hearts knows what the mind of the Spirit is, because He **makes intercession** for the saints according to the will of God.*

> **Make intercession** - *entunchano /en-toong-khan-oh/*: to fall in with, meet with in order to converse.

From this description of a casual encounter, the word progresses to the idea of pleading with a person on behalf of another, although at times, the petition may be against another[33].

---

[33] Source: New Spirit Filled Life Bible - Jack W. Hayford, p. 1737

But now I am going to Jerusalem to minister to the saints. For it pleased those from Macedonia and Achaia to make a certain **_contribution_** *for the poor among the saints who are in Jerusalem.*

> **Contribution/fellowship** - *koinonia /koy-nohn-ee-ah/*: sharing, unity, close association, partnership, participation, a society, a communion, a fellowship, contributory help, the brotherhood.

Koinonia is a unity brought about by the Holy Spirit. In *koinonia* the individual shares in common an intimate bond of fellowship with the rest of the Christian society. *Koinonia* cements the believers to the Lord Jesus and to each other[34].

Now I beg you, brethren, through the Lord Jesus Christ, and through the love of the Spirit, that you strive together with me in prayers to God for me, that I may be delivered from those in Judea who do not believe, and that my service for Jerusalem may be acceptable to the saints…

Greet Philologus and Julia, Nereus and his sister, and Olympas, and all the saints who are with them.

To the church of God which is at Corinth, to those who are sanctified in Christ Jesus, called to be saints, with all who in every place call on the name of Jesus Christ our Lord, both theirs and ours:

---

[34] Source: New Spirit Filled Life Bible - Jack W. Hayford, p. 1494

This verse shows that those called saints are sanctified in Christ Jesus.

1 Corinthians 6:1–2

Dare any of you, having a matter against another, go to law before the unrighteous, and not before the saints? Do you not know that the saints will judge the world? And if the world will be judged by you, are you unworthy to judge the smallest matters?

Here, Paul is saying to the believers that when they have a problem with one another, they should try to solve it amongst themselves. I believe it must have been that they were used to going to non-believers to settle their disputes at that time. But Paul means to say that as believers, they have a community of people guided by the Holy Spirit, who is full of wisdom and well able to settle their argument.

1 Corinthians 14:33

For God is not the author of confusion but of peace, as in all the churches of the saints.

1 Corinthians 16:1

Now concerning the collection for the saints, as I have given orders to the churches of Galatia, so you must do also:

1 Corinthians 16:15 (NKJV)

I urge you, brethren—you know the household of Stephanas, that it is the firstfruits of Achaia, and that they have devoted themselves to the ministry of the saints...

1 Corinthians 16:15 (NLT)

You know that Stephanas and his household were the first of the harvest of believers in Greece, and they are spending their lives in service to God's people…

We read that there was devotion to the ministry of the saints.

2 Corinthians 8:3–4 (NKJV)

*For I bear **witness** that according to their ability, yes, and beyond their ability, they were freely willing, imploring us with much urgency that we would receive the gift and the fellowship of the ministering to the saints.*

> **Witnessing** - *martureo /mar-too-reh-oh/:* giving evidence, attesting, confirming, confessing, bearing record, speaking well of, giving a good report, testifying, affirming that one has seen, heard, or experienced something.

In the New Testament, it is used to present the gospel with evidence. The English word 'martyr' comes from this word, suggesting that a witness is one willing to die for his testimony[35].

2 Corinthians 8:3–4 (NLT)

For I can testify that they gave not only what they could afford, but far more. And they did it of their own free will. They begged us again and again for the privilege of sharing in the gift for the believers in Jerusalem.

---

[35] Source: New Spirit Filled Life Bible - Jack W. Hayford, p. 1539

2 Corinthians 9:12 (NKJV)

*For the administration of this **service** not only supplies the needs of the saints, but also is abounding through many thanksgivings to God,*

> **Service** - *leitourgia /lie-toorg-ee-ah/*: from laos 'people' and ergon 'work'.

The word was originally used for citizens serving in public office at their own expense. Later it included military service or community participation. In the New Testament, *leitourgia* is used both for priestly service and unselfish giving. In 2 Corinthians 9:12, it denotes charitable gifts as a service to the needy[36].

2 Corinthians 9:12 (NLT)

So two good things will result from this ministry of giving—the needs of the believers in Jerusalem will be met, and they will joyfully express their thanks to God.

Ephesians 1:18

*The eyes of your **understanding** being enlightened; that you may know what is the hope of His calling, what are the riches of the glory of His inheritance in the saints…*

> **Understanding/mind** - *dianoia /dee-an-oy-ah/*: literally 'a thinking through'.

Dianoia combines *nous*, 'mind', and *dia* 'through'. The word suggests understanding, insight, meditation, reflection, perception, the gift of apprehension, and the faculty of thought. When this

---

[36] Source: New Spirit Filled Life Bible - Jack W. Hayford, p. 1385

faculty is renewed by the Holy Spirit, the whole mindset changes from the fearful negativism of the carnal mind to the vibrant, positive thinking of the quickened spiritual mind[37].

This verse tells us that **in the saints**, we have an inheritance. This means that we cannot say we are believers and not go to a local church. The word tells us that there is an inheritance in our fellow brothers and sisters. We will be missing something when we decide not to be part of a local church.

Ephesians 2:19

Now, therefore, you are no longer strangers and foreigners, but fellow citizens with the saints and members of the household of God, 20 having been built on the foundation of the apostles and prophets, Jesus Christ Himself being the chief cornerstone…

Ephesians 3:14–18

*For this reason I bow my knees to the Father of our Lord Jesus Christ, 15 from whom the whole family in heaven and earth is named, 16 that He would **grant** you, according to the riches of His glory, to be strengthened with might through His Spirit in the inner man, 17 that Christ may dwell in your hearts through faith; that you, being rooted and grounded in love, 18 may be able to **comprehend** with all the saints what is the width and length and depth and height— 19 to **know** the love of Christ which passes knowledge; that you may be filled with all the **fullness** of God.*

Grant/give - *didomi /did-oh-mee/:* granting, allowing, bestowing, imparting, permitting, placing, offering, presenting, yielding, and paying.

---

[37] Source: New Spirit Filled Life Bible - Jack W. Hayford, p. 1373

Didomi implies giving an object of value. It gives freely and is unforced. Jesus did not say it would be more natural or easier to give than to receive, but it would be more blessed[38].

> **Comprehend** - *katalambano /kat-al-am-ban-oh/*: the word is capable of three interpretations
> 1 To seize, lay hold of, overcome.
> 2 To perceive, attain, lay hold of with the mind; to apprehend with mental or moral effort.
> 3 To quench, extinguish, snuff out the light by stifling it.

> **Know** - *ginosko /ghin-oce-koe/*: to perceive, understand, recognize, gain knowledge, realize, come to know.

Ginosk is the knowledge that has an inception, a progress, and an attainment. It is the recognition of truth by personal experience[39].

> **Fullness** - *pleroma /play-row-mah/*: full number, full complement, full measure, copiousness, plenitude, that which has been completed.

The word describes a ship with full cargo and crew and a town with no empty houses. Pleroma strongly emphasizes fullness and completion[40].

---

[38] Filled Source: New Spirit Life Bible - Jack W. Hayford, p. 1530
[39] Source: New Spirit Filled Life Bible - Jack W. Hayford, p. 1443, 1459
[40] Source: New Spirit Filled Life Bible - Jack W. Hayford, p. 1649

These words are so rich. It was Paul's prayer for the Ephesians, but let it also be our prayer today. That in faith, we might gain an understanding of the amazing love of God and be aware that we have received the fullness of God.

Ephesians 4:11–12

And He Himself gave some to be apostles, some prophets, some evangelists, and some pastors and teachers, for the equipping of the saints for the work of ministry, for the edifying of the body of Christ…

Ephesians 6:18

Praying always with all prayer and supplication in the Spirit, being watchful to this end with all perseverance and supplication for all the saints…

We ought to pray for the saints. When you are tempted to complain about your brothers and sisters, pray for them. Confront them when needed, but pray for them because we cannot change people, but God can.

Colossians 1:12

Giving thanks to the Father who has qualified us to be partakers of the inheritance of the saints in the light.

Colossians 1:24–26

*I now rejoice in my sufferings for you, and fill up in my flesh what is lacking in the afflictions of Christ, for the sake of His body, which is the church, of which I became a minister according to the stewardship from God which was given to me for you, to fulfill the word of God, the **mystery** which has been hidden from ages and from generations, but now has been revealed to His saints.*

In the New Testament, the word denotes something that people could never know by their own understanding and that demands a revelation from God. The secret thoughts, plans, and dispensations of God remain hidden from unregenerate mankind but are revealed to all believers. In non-biblical Greek, *musterion* is knowledge withheld, concealed, or silenced. In biblical Greek, it is truth revealed. The New Testament *musterion* focuses on Christ's sinless life, atoning death, powerful resurrection, and dynamic ascension[41].

It was concealed for a long time, but in the time of Paul, it was revealed to the saints what God's plan had been all along, which was to restore mankind back to a relationship with Him, the heavenly Father.

---

[41] Source: New Spirit Filled Life Bible - Jack W. Hayford, p. 1356

Leadership in the church

The Bible provides us with guidelines for a lot of church matters. There's enough we can find in the Word when it comes to leadership. Below are some characteristics we should find in leaders:

- Leaders have authority that is given to them by God for the edification of the people (2 Corinthians 10:8).
- A leader is a servant. A leader has a record of being a servant to other leaders. (Examples: Moses to Jethro, Joshua to Moses.)
- A leader is a steward (1 Corinthians 4:1).
- A leader is faithful (1 Corinthians 4:2).
- A leader is obedient (Luke 12:42–43).

Titus 1:7–9

*For a bishop must be blameless, as a **steward** of God, not self-willed, not quick-tempered, not given to wine, not violent, not greedy for money, but hospitable, a lover of what is good, sober-minded, just, holy, self-controlled, holding fast the faithful word as he has been taught, that he may be able, by **sound doctrine**, both to exhort and convict those who contradict.*

Steward - *oikonomos/oy-kon-om-oss/*: from oikos, 'house', a nemo, 'to arrange'.

The word originally referred to the manager of a household or estate. In a broader sense, it denoted an administrator or steward in general. In 1 Corinthians 4 and Titus 1:7, it refers to Christian

*We ought to pray for the saints.
When you are tempted to complain
about your brothers and sisters,
pray for them. Confront them when
needed, but pray for them because we
cannot change people, but God can.*

ministers, but in 1 Peter 4:10, it denotes Christians in general, using the gifts entrusted to them by the Lord for the strengthening and encouragement of fellow believers. [42]

Metaphorically, the word refers to sound doctrine, sound words, and soundness in the faith[43].

- A servant leader is a good steward of the manifold grace of God (1 Peter 4:10).
- A leader's courage is built by receiving encouragement, and a leader builds courage in others by encouraging them.
- A leader has a God-given vision (Habakkuk 2:2–3).
- Leaders are generous (2 Corinthians 9:7).
- Leaders have the ministry of reconciliation (2 Corinthians 5:14–21).
- Leaders have the fear of the Lord.

1 Timothy 3:1–13

*This is a faithful saying: If a man desires the position of a bishop, he **desires** a good work. A bishop then must be blameless, the husband of one wife, temperate, sober-minded, of good behavior, hospitable, able to teach; not given to wine, not violent, not greedy for money, but **gentle**, not quarrelsome, not covetous; one who rules his own house well, having his children in submission with all reverence (for if a man*

---

[42] Source: New Spirit Filled Life Bible - Jack W. Hayford, p. 1768
[43] Source: New Spirit Filled Life Bible - Jack W. Hayford, p. 1797

*does not know how to rule his own house, how will he take care of the church of God?); not a novice, lest being puffed up with pride he fall into the same condemnation as the devil. Moreover, he must have a good testimony among those who are outside, lest he fall into reproach and the snare of the devil. Likewise, deacons must be **reverent**, not double-tongued, not given to much wine, not greedy for money, holding the **mystery** of the faith with a pure conscience. But let these also first be tested; then let them serve as deacons, being found blameless. Likewise, their wives must be reverent, not slanderers, temperate, faithful in all things. Let deacons be the husbands of one wife, ruling their children and their own houses well. For those who have served well as deacons obtain for themselves a good standing and great **boldness** in the faith which is in Christ Jesus.*

> **Desires** - *epithumeo/ep-ee-thoo-meh-oh/*: to set one's heart upon, eagerly long for, covet, greatly desire, lust after.

The worde pithumeo emphasizes the intensity of the desire rather than the object desired. It describes both good and evil desires.[44]

> **Gentle** - *epieikes/ep-ee-eye-kace/*: from epi, 'unto', and eikos, 'likely'.

The word *"epieikes"* suggests a character that is equitable, reasonable, forbearing, moderate, fair, and considerate. It is the opposite of harsh, abrasive, sarcastic, cruel, and contentious. The person with *epieikes* does not insist on the letter of the law[45].

---

[44] Source: New Spirit Filled Life Bible - Jack W. Hayford, p. 1314
[45] Source: New Spirit Filled Life Bible - Jack W. Hayford, p. 1702

Leaders in the church should set a good example by displaying a deportment that commands respect. Since *semnos* is used by both husband and wife, an idealistic attractiveness should characterize all Christian couples.

Parrhesia also refers to a clear presentation of the gospel without being ambiguous or unintelligible. Parrhesia is not a human quality but a result of being filled with the Holy Spirit[46].

- A leader is humble.
- Leaders show vulnerability.
- Leaders lead God's way.
- Leaders take charge when it's needed.
- A leader is accountable.

I believe that most leaders in the world and the church have a certain charisma. It makes them attract many people, and this plays a great role when people choose a church to go to. From my point of view, there's nothing wrong with that, but we must look for other traits in a leader. Besides their gifts, we must also look at their character. I'm not talking about perfection, because

---

[46] Source: New Spirit Filled Life Bible - Jack W. Hayford, pp. 1702, 1497

nobody is perfect. In the kingdom of God, everyone is growing and allowed to make mistakes. As congregants, we must not put such a high standard on leaders that we write them off when they make mistakes. Yes, they have a greater responsibility, but they are humans too. They are not God; only God is without mistakes. Leaders must be humble enough to accept their mistakes and be willing to right their wrongs.

From my personal experience, there is one thing in the lives of all believers that is indispensable, and that is accountability. We see this modeled in the life of Jesus. Jesus gave us the perfect example when He said that whatever He did, He first saw the Father do. Jesus was accountable to God the Father. Like this, we must be accountable in the church too. Leaders must have people to be accountable to—people who can guide them and correct them.

With the knowledge and wisdom I have now, I would say that if I were placed before choosing a church, one of the questions I would ask the leader(s) is: Who are you accountable to? It's not that I think we need babysitters or anything of the sort, but as I said earlier, we are not perfect or exempt from mistakes. I believe it is God's will for church leaders to be accountable to other leaders. Being accountable also helps a church leader receive guidance, especially when he/she is inexperienced.

To continue my experience, which is still in progress, I would say that it is not easy to truly be a committed member of a church, but it is really worth it. As I write this, I am still a member of the church I was talking about at the beginning of the book, and I can say that I'm still growing.

Looking back, I can say that it is easy to go to a church because of the strength we see in that particular church. But we must be aware that there will never be a perfect church because a church consists of people who make mistakes. So sooner or later, something will happen that will place you with the option of leaving. We must realize that being part of a church is for the establishment of the kingdom of God. Being part of a church is for our maturation as sons of God to become good representatives of God, our Father.

We must realize that going to church on its own is not a goal. We cannot say we have arrived because we go to church every Sunday. The church is supposed to be a training place that shows us who the Father is, who we are in the Father, and how we can represent the Father correctly.

Experiencing disappointment

God created the church to be a safe place for His children to grow. It could be that when you look around, you don't see any church you could consider a safe place. I can say that it is hard to believe in the church again. Or, better said, believe in the people in the church again. It is something you cannot do without God. When you have experienced hurt in the church, no one can convince you to trust again—only God. It will boil down to trusting God that whatever happens, He is able to heal and restore.

People will disappoint us; still, it is not a reason not to be part of a church. Do we think we are so superhuman that we will never disappoint others? We need to be wise, though. Don't be afraid to ask questions. Remember that in a moment of excitement, you can commit to everything, but there will come times when the excitement is far from being found. Does that mean that it's time to leave? No, not if that is the house God has called you to be part of.

You may say, "But I can read my Bible at home and watch online church. That is my spiritual food." Let me remind you there is more to the church than giving you the word. The leaders to care for your soul. They pray for you, counsel you, and guide you. There is only so far that the online church can go. If a church leader does not have a way to know you and your family physically, he/she is not your spiritual leader.

How to leave a church?

These past couple of years have taught me about leaving a church. I've experienced leaving a church and even witnessed the dissolution of another. I must admit that I initially did not handle it very well either. On our journey, a lot can happen. It might be that we don't feel at home in a church. I've observed that when the tipping point is reached, and the decision is already settled, people tend to communicate this to the church leaders. Whenever I decide to stop going to a particular church, I inform the leaders. From what I know now, I can say there is a better way to do this. Often, there is a whole process that precedes a decision like this. I believe that it would be good for the person in question to involve the leaders in this and talk about it, and maybe something can be done before it comes down to them leaving the church.

It can also be that the church cannot provide what you are expecting. Then the question becomes, "Are you willing to wait until your need or desire can be met?" If we are honest, most of the time, what happens is that we miss something in a particular church, and that feeling or idea becomes stronger. Sometimes, we find another church that seems to provide what we miss in our current church and decide to leave. Then, we leave or communicate to the leaders that we are leaving. I believe you can leave a church if the leaders can never provide for your needs and cannot help you get there.

The leaders placed over you are to care for your soul. They pray for you, counsel you, and guide you. There is only so far that the online church can go. If a church leader does not have a way to know you and your family physically, he/she is not your spiritual leader.

I believe there is an ideal way, though. Between the feeling of starting to miss something and deciding to leave is a big gap. At this point, a conversation should start between the person thinking about leaving and the leaders to find the best solution.

I believe that the church should be a training ground. Therefore, for a certain period, you will be trained so that you will be ready to be sent out to expand the work of the kingdom elsewhere, and you will be sent out with the blessing of your leaders, who will become your overseers. And the process starts again. By "sent out," I don't only mean sent out to start a church. We can be ready to be sent out in our workplace, and we, in turn, can teach, preach, and demonstrate the kingdom there.

Conclusion

When I look back at the questions that started me on this journey, I can say that I discovered that the church is not something
we, as humans, came up with. The church was part of God's
plan; it was not an afterthought. Jesus gave His life and shed His
blood for the church. Thanks to His sacrifice, the church was
born. His intention for the church is to be a place where people
will find Him. A place where people can find the truth. A place
where people can be formed into the image of Christ. A place
of sound teaching to mature the people so they are ready for the
work that will advance His kingdom.

We can experience a lot in and with a church. In my experience,
there is always a way out—a solution. I do not minimize any bad
experience someone may have had. The truth remains that the
church should not be thrown away because of bad experiences.
I agree that it should not be the place where people get hurt.
Sadly, that is a reality. But the truth remains that the church is
the vehicle that God has chosen. It remains that it is a place that
should be a haven, a place where we share good and bad times
together. A place where we should be trained, where we should
mature, and where we should contribute. We cannot believe the

lie that we can serve and believe in God and not be part of a community of believers; we need community.

We may leave a certain church, but we should know there is a right way to do so. We are supposed to be planted in a house, grow roots, and become stable trees that bear good fruit.

At the end of this book, I want to challenge you to look at your situation in the church. Is it the church, as described in the Bible, that you don't believe in or the people who disappointed you? I want to challenge you to look for a way to reconcile with the true idea of the church. That idea has not changed. There is a place where you belong. Don't give up just yet.

The church is still worth a shot because it is part of God's eternal plan, and there are those who, with a sincere heart, are willing to let God form them and use them in the process.

Biography

"What about the church?" is the first book written by Suhaina. She has always had a fascination for the written word and reading. Besides that, she has a passion for the Word of God and believes that it is an enrichment to her writings.

Together with her husband, Swendly, Suhaina serves as an elder and pastor at the local church, Heaven Designed Life. Together with the team of elders, she has been instrumental in building the local church on the blueprint portrayed in the Bible.

Born on the island of Curaçao and now living in the Netherlands, she became the colorful woman she is today.